PLEASE DON'T ASK ME TO SING IN THE CHOIR

by Thomas L. Are

ONE MINUTE REFLECTIONS
FOR THE CHURCH CHOIR

Hope
Publishing Company
CAROL STREAM   IL 60188

Copyright © 1985 by Hope Publishing Company.
International Copyright Secured. All Rights Reserved.
Printed in the United States of America.
ISBN 0-916642-28-3

INTRODUCTION

"I need help," he said.

"What can I do for you?" I replied, trying to hide the flattery I felt. Every church leader knew his reputation as a minister of music, and he was calling me from over a thousand miles away. I knew that no matter what he wanted, I would help him.

"Where can I find devotionals that relate to a choir . . . and not too long?"

I couldn't help him. I knew exactly what he wanted but neither of us knew where to find them.

Most church musicians hunger to claim the spiritual aspect of our work. We know it's there but few of us feel comfortable expressing our faith in words. The choir director who called me said, "I feel the choir thinks I'm playing preacher when I talk about God. I need some help."

PLEASE DON'T ASK ME TO SING tells of sixty experiences and reflections of a choir singer. Most of these are my own. Even though I now serve as a pastor, for years my growth as a Christian came through singing in a church choir.

I seek in these pages to affirm those of you who still sing. Your ministry of music enhances the total mission of the church. Many of us are indebted to you.

QUOTES FROM R.S.V.

DEDICATED TO THE MEMORY OF JACK CHAMBLESS WHOSE DEDICATION TO THE CHURCH CHOIR WAS SELDOM OUT OF THE AUTHOR'S MIND IN THE WRITING OF THIS BOOK.

CONTENTS

INTRODUCTION
1. BECAUSE I WANT TO — 1
2. NOT SURE I BELONG — 3
3. WHAT A PHONY — 5
4. IN OVER MY HEAD — 7
5. GOD REALLY IS HERE — 9
6. PRAISE DESERVES A SACRIFICE — 11
7. THE SHOW OFF — 13
8. TOO TIRED TO STAY HOME — 15
9. WHY DO I DO IT? — 17
10. BRING OUT MELODY — 19
11. PROUD TO BE A HYPOCRITE — 21
12. SPEAK TO ONE ANOTHER — 23
13. HELP, THEY ARE CRITICIZING ME! — 25
14. I'M LATE AGAIN — 27
15. SURPRISED BY WORSHIP — 29
16. REMEMBER WHEN? — 31
17. GRIPES OR GRATITUDE? — 33
18. INSTANT EVERYTHING — 35
19. FRIENDLY HABITS — 37
20. DO IT AGAIN — 39
21. SURPRISED BY REWARD — 41
22. FAITH, REGARDLESS — 43
23. THE HOPE OF DEATH — 45
24. BECKY QUIT — 47
25. INTERRUPTED SCHEDULES — 49
26. ONLY ONE EXPRESSION — 51
27. REACTION TO GRACE — 53
28. DOING WHAT I CAN — 55
29. DEALING WITH ANGER — 57
30. THE RISK OF NOT GIVING — 59
31. FALLING OUT OF EDEN — 61
32. FEELING FORGIVEN — 63
33. WORRY TRAP — 65
34. GOD WITHIN — 67
35. OUR VISUAL MESSAGE — 69
36. GIVE ME PATIENCE, NOW — 71
37. GOD CALLS IN A WHISPER — 73
38. SAM'S GOAL IS DEATH — 75
39. I HATE TO SAY "I'M SORRY" — 77
40. GOD, SHE MUST BE LONELY! — 79

41.	THOSE WHO HOLD ME	81
42.	EMOTIONAL FREEDOM	83
43.	WHEN DEPRESSION COMES	85
44.	I NEED YOU TO LISTEN	87
45.	WHERE ARE THE ROADSIGNS?	89
46.	MAXIMUM LIVING	91
47.	WHEN THE LIGHTS GO OUT	93
48.	YEAH, THAT'S WHAT I SAY!	95
49.	DANCE A LITTLE	97
50.	GOD'S RHYTHM	99
51.	THE RISK OF BEING THERE	101
52.	ON SAYING GOODBYE	103
53.	THANKSGIVING – A MATTER OF FAITH	105
54.	CHRISTMAS – RUSH, RUSH, RUSH	107
55.	NEW YEAR'S – ONE DAY AT A TIME	109
56.	EPIPHANY – GOING HOME DIFFERENT	111
57.	MISSIONS – IMPRACTICAL	113
58.	PALM SUNDAY – EXPECTING TOO LITTLE	115
59.	EASTER – OUR BIG ONE	117
60.	PENTECOST – THE SPIRIT AMONG US	119

Chapter 1

BECAUSE I WANT TO

> "So will I ever sing praises to thy name, as I pay my vows day after day."
> PSALM 61:8

"I'm thinking about joining the choir at church."

"Oh . . . I don't know if that's a good idea. It would tie us down on the weekends," my wife, Ellen, said.

"Yeah, I know. I've thought about that and I've thought of other things, too. Going to rehearsals when tired, being away from home another night each week, not sitting with you and the kids in church. But it's something I think I would like to do," I said, talking more to myself than to her.

"You're serious, aren't you? I didn't know you had such a good voice," she sounded more surprised than opposed to the idea.

The next Thursday, I felt a little surprised myself walking into choir rehearsal. I could think of a hundred reasons to be somewhere else but over against all the reasonable objections, something inside me wanted to give it a try.

I learned something about myself. I usually wind up doing things I *want to do*. I do my work and volunteer my services because of an inner desire.

My wants may be the lesser of two evils. I may not desire to get up each morning but I choose to be a responsible person so I do. I will make sacrifices to sing in the choir and my family will too, but only because I want to do it.

I think God leads me in this way. Every time I have been called to serve Him, He has accompanied the opportunity with a desire to do it.

Maybe this is one way the Holy Spirit works in us. At least for me, when it feels right and it seems good with God, I believe He has His hand in it. I will take seriously my choir commitment, making my vow not only to the church, but also to God Himself.

The psalmist said, "So will I ever sing praises to thy name, as I pay my vows day after day." I'll do that too, because I want to.

PRAYER: Lord, guide me in my choices. And now that I have made the commitment to sing in the choir, help me to be faithful.

In Christ,
Amen.

Chapter 2

NOT SURE I BELONG

> "And when Jesus came to the place, he looked up and said to him, 'Zacchaeus, make haste and come down; for I must stay at your house today.' So he made haste and came down, and received him joyfully. And when they saw it they all murmured, 'He has gone in to be the guest of a man who is a sinner'."
>
> LUKE 19:5-7

A month after joining the choir, I still felt I did not belong.

Three rehearsals and two services hardly qualified me as a veteran but I should be comfortable by now. The other choir members have welcomed me and several in the congregation expressed appreciation for my singing. I always get along with people and look forward to a closer fellowship with this group. Yet I am troubled. The problem is me.

Reverend Tom Walker, our pastor, made a statement from the pulpit that surprised me. "I am convinced that most of you sitting in pews are feeling two things. First, you are saying to yourselves, 'If these church people really knew me, they wouldn't like me.' Second, most of you feel, 'I'm the only one here who feels this way'." He continued to talk about the unworthiness most of us felt. Suddenly I realized why I felt so uneasy.

The *image* disturbs me. People have a way of saying, "He's a big church member, even sings in the choir."

Well, I'm no saint. I believe in God and want to serve Him, but if they are looking for a sample of Christ-likeness, they'll have to look beyond me. In fact, according to Reverend Walker, they'll have to look beyond the whole church. We're not here because we're worthy but because we're grateful. God accepts us as we are. So I belong here. My unworthiness qualifies me for a group that expresses thanksgiving to the God who welcomes us.

In my search to belong, I feel like Zacchaeus, called out of self-consciousness into God's fellowship and service. If you sing in a choir, I bet you do, too.

PRAYER: Lord, thank you for accepting us when we feel so unacceptable, and thank you for giving us one another.
In Christ,
Amen.

Chapter 3

WHAT A PHONY

> "I do not understand my own actions. For I do not do what I want, but I do the very thing I hate."
> ROMANS 7:15

"Be careful," David, our director said. "The second measure after you turn the page is tricky."

We all looked at it. Immediately I knew I was in trouble. I couldn't read the notes and the rhythm threw me.

"Let's clap it through now so we'll have the feel of it when we get there," David said.

For five minutes, we clapped to rhythm until David was sure we all had it, but I knew I was going to miss it. I felt it in my bones. We sang okay on the first page. David cautioned us just before turning the page. "Be careful now, the tough part is coming up." I turned the page, anticipated, waited, and missed it. David cast his eyes at me but the choir kept on singing. He had given me all the help he could and I should have done it better.

A moment later, David stopped us. "It's all right to make a mistake," he said, "in fact, when in doubt, shout. If you let me hear it, we can correct it."

Since that time I have thought of David's advice. I often get anxious and fail. I don't hear my kids because I'm impatient; I let others down because I'm careless; and I claim credits that I don't deserve because I'm insecure. Yesterday I hurt a friend. I excused it by telling myself I was just tired, but I regret what I said. I wish now that I could take it back, but how can I? Sometimes the things

I regret doing are much more serious, for like Paul "I do not do what I want, but I do the very thing I hate."

Thank God for the church. I need a place for those who fail. Here I don't have to deny my human frailty and every week I hear of God's forgiveness. What a phony I would be without this place and that message.

PRAYER: Lord, when we fail others, show us a better way. Give us more concern for serving You than for condemning ourselves.

      In Christ,
      Amen.

Chapter 4

IN OVER MY HEAD

> "For as the heavens are higher than the earth, so are my ways higher than your ways and my thoughts than your thoughts."
>
> ISAIAH 55:9

At first I thought, " Buxtehude! Why would David choose such hard music? It's over our heads. I liked the anthem we sang last week, sweet and simple. But Buxtehude, ugh! who understands it? Where's the melody?"

I don't always comprehend the sermon either. In fact, a lot of worship challenges me. I guess I don't like being stretched. It would be nicer if everything about God's message was familiar and comfortable. I enjoy the things that fit me like an old shoe.

Yet I know God is awesome. His thoughts are above our thoughts and His ways are above our ways. Who can understand God? Or more significant than that, would I stand in awe of God if I could understand Him? Would I praise Him if He were not a mystery?

I am grateful for the incomprehensibleness of God, for profound thoughts and even for Buxtehude. I may groan but I'm glad God does not appeal to the least common denominator in us. If God were easy, if I ever get Him dissected and analyzed, then what would happen to faith? Relating to God always rests on faith.

Sometimes I think I would swap all my faith for one little ounce of certainty. Yet if my mind could contain God, He wouldn't be God.

I'm caught in a paradox. God gave me a mind and expects me to use it, but He also lets me know that He is beyond my limits. Everytime I try to understand God, I wade in over my head and I am glad. I can believe in and praise such a God—beyond me.

PRAYER: Lord, we thank you that we can relate to You by our praise and not have to depend upon our understanding. Help us to express our doxology with more certainty than our theology.
                                          In Christ,
                                          Amen.

Chapter 5

GOD REALLY IS HERE

> "For where two or three are gathered in my name, there am I in the midst of them."
> MATTHEW 18:20

Sunday morning, eleven o'clock, worship begins:
"The Lord is in His holy Temple.
Let all the earth keep silent before Him."

We sang those words last week and the three weeks before that. I've heard them all my life and they have never disturbed me before. Why now? Something about God's being here with us frightens me. It's one thing to say it. It's another thing to believe it. God really is here.

The Bible speaks often of God's presence in the cloud, the tabernacle and the temple. Especially in Jesus, God came to be with us. Yet all of these records of God's presence refer to a time back then and somewhere else.

Our call to worship declares that God is here with us now. Of course God is everywhere and always with us. He lives in the shop at midafternoon as surely as in the sanctuary at eleven o'clock. It's just that I'm not as aware of Him in those busy times as I am in the quiet of the here and now. The architecture and symbols of this sanctuary, the prelude and gathering of our congregation enable me to feel His presence. The Lord *is* in His holy temple. No wonder I'm anxious. These words are more than a song; they proclaim a truth.

It's one thing to believe in God; that He exists and is holy, just and loving. But to worship Him, I must feel His presence. "Where two or three are gathered together in my name, there I am in the midst of them," becomes more than a promise to be believed. It's a reality I experience.

PRAYER: Lord, help us to feel Your presence as we worship. Fill our emotions with faith.
In Christ,
Amen.

Chapter 6

PRAISE DESERVES A SACRIFICE

> "Through him then let us continually offer up a sacrifice of praise to God, that is, the fruit of lips that acknowledge his name. Do not neglect to do good and to share what you have, for such sacrifices are pleasing to God."
> HEBREWS 13:15-16

Pick the scriptures on almost any page and we find praise wedded to sacrifice.

I enjoy praise. It's fun to sing. But I seldom think of sacrifice. Oh, I go to rehearsals when I am tired. Some weekends give way to choir responsibilities. Becoming involved in church activities motivates me to give money. Sometimes I even give up time with my family to do church work. But sacrifice? That word is too strong for the kind of things I do.

Most of the biblical prophets and saints walked roads of toil and torture. Early Christians suffered martyrdom for their faith. On the other hand, I grumble because the rehearsal room gets hot. My sacrifices are small.

Yet even my small offerings praise God.

Too often I underestimate the importance of my sacrifices, for instance, the faithfulness I show in attending choir. If I don't go to rehearsal tonight, it will be twice as easy to skip next week. Then I'll soon go only when convenient or when nothing else seems more enticing. When I take my choir commitment casually, others will too and I become a bad example.

"You're here every week, aren't you?" Cecil asked. "Don't you ever feel tempted to skip choir and stay home?"

"Oh, yes, but a good choir enhances worship and that's important. It deserves a sacrifice."

Maybe this reflects what the writer to the Hebrews meant, "Then let us continually offer up a sacrifice of praise to God, that is, the fruit of lips that acknowledge His name."

Of course, the sacrifice God wants most . . . is me.

PRAYER: Lord, help us take seriously our opportunity to serve You. Use our voices, but most of all use the example we set.

                                            In Christ,
                                            Amen.

Chapter 7

THE SHOW OFF

> "For by the grace given to me I bid every one among you not to think of himself more highly than he ought to think, but to think with sober judgment, each according to the measure of faith which God has assigned him."
> ROMANS 12:3

"Lord, make me invisible." That's what I used to pray. Someone had convinced me that I could not point to Christ and also draw attention to myself at the same time. So I tried to be inconspicuous. I never made it. The harder I tried, the less it worked. The more humble I determined to be, the more self-centered I became.

Now I pray, "Lord, turn me on for you." I believe God speaks through personalities, voices, eyes and faces. He makes Himself known even through me, so I want to do my best.

Yet my ego presents a danger. That flashy bass part in this week's anthem tempts me to gloat in the sound of it. It fits my voice so well that I may sing to show off. I confess a mixture of boastfulness in everything I do well.

A greater danger would be in self-abasement. What an inverted arrogance when I'm proud of my humility. A "Hold me back, Lord . . . if you let me go, I may be too much," may be the kind of subtle boasting Paul had in mind when he said, "I bid everyone among you not to think of himself more highly than he ought to think."

Paul goes on to say in this same passage, "Having gifts that differ according to the grace given to us, let us use them."

Every gift comes from God. As long as I recognize that He gave them to be used, then I am free to enjoy my talents and do my best.

PRAYER: Lord, deliver us from false humility. Use all that we are and can do for your glory.
                                        In Christ,
                                        Amen.

Chapter 8

TOO TIRED TO STAY HOME

> "Take my yoke upon you, and learn from me; for I am gentle and lowly in heart, and you will find rest for your souls."
> MATTHEW 11:29

It happens to me so often that I have come to expect it. I come home from work tired, go to rehearsal tired, and come home from choir refreshed.

On some days, work seems long. Fighting the homebound traffic leaves me dragging into the house determined to kick up my feet and stay there. Then Ellen says, "Don't get too comfortable, remember you have choir practice tonight." Every bone in my body cries, "Oh, no, not tonight."

Thirty minutes later, I'm sharing greetings with friends. We sing through half a dozen anthems. My body pulses to rhythms and vibrates with sound. My heart responds to the texts we sing. In two hours, I'm a new man. My tired body has been refreshed. It happens every time!

Sometimes I think the recreation of singing provides enough diversion from life's routines to affect the body like a vacation. Jesus said, "Take my yoke . . . and you will find rest." I believe in today's world the yoke of Christ is the work of the church. Serving Him brings with it God's promise of rest. Does that mean that the choir is a therapy group? Yes, I think it is, not because choir members are trained therapists but because we are a people serving God together. When we carry the Lord's yoke, He becomes our counselor.

Sometimes when it's time for choir, I'm just too tired to stay home.

PRAYER: Lord, help us to burn ourselves out for you, that we may know peace. Rest us in your service.
In Christ,
Amen.

Chapter 9

WHY DO I DO IT?

> "May you be strengthened with all power, according to his glorious might, for all endurance and patience with joy, giving thanks to the Father, who has qualified us to share in the inheritance of the saints in light."
> COLOSSIANS 1:11-12

"Today is a special day," Reverend Tom Walker announced. "We recognize with appreciation our Sunday school teachers. Please stand as I call your name."

We had heard a sermon on Christian education, each teacher had been given a certificate and now as I sit in the choir, I watch them all take bows. Perhaps I am jealous. Choir singers never receive such recognition. We work just as hard, serve as faithfully, and have never been offered a rotation system. Why aren't we equally appreciated?

I'm engaging in a bit of self-pity but sometimes I ask, why do I do it? For the congregation? I don't think so. I feel good when someone compliments me or says he enjoys the music, but I don't do it for their appreciation. I don't even do it for God's appreciation, though I hope He is pleased with what I do.

I sing in the choir for two reasons. First, because I appreciate God. It's one way I have to say "thank you" to Him. I'm grateful and need to express my gratitude.

Second, I sing in the choir because I enjoy it. It's fun to sing, and music touches me on a level deeper than words either spoken or read. In the choir, I come alive and feel in touch with my world.

Maybe that's the greatest value I have, my own self-appreciation. That may be part of what Paul had in mind when He prayed for the Colossians, "giving thanks to the Father who has qualified us to share in the inheritance of the saints in light."

PRAYER: Lord, somewhere between self-worship and the feeling that I'm no good lies a balance for a useful, Godly life. Help me to find it.
．．．．．．．．．．．．．．．．．．．．．．．．．．．In Christ,
．．．．．．．．．．．．．．．．．．．．．．．．．．．Amen.

Chapter 10

BRING OUT THE MELODY

> "We must work the works of him who sent me, while it is day; night comes, when no one can work."
> JOHN 9:4

"Bring out the melody," David yelled as we sang. "Listen for the melody. If you can't hear it, you're singing too loud."

Later, reflecting on David's instructions to the choir, I thought how similar to life. Music moves through a series of discords and resolutions creating a melody. Life is like that.

Some of us spend most of our time each day solving one incidental problem after another, seeking resolutions to discord. But that's not enough. Music and life must lead somewhere. To have melody, they both must move toward something, to tell a story and have a goal.

I ask myself, what's the main theme of my life? Is it solving daily problems, or am I committed to long-range goals? If so, then do I allow other sounds to crowd the tune of my life? In the choir all the sounds are good, even essential, unless they cover up the melody.

Just last week a friend invited me to play golf on Sunday. I wanted the recreation and saw it as an opportunity for fellowship. Nothing wrong with it, except I've committed my Sundays to worship. Golf would cover up the main theme of my life.

Sometimes all of us allow noises much less wholesome than recreation to ruin our time. We listen to worry, anxiety and guilt until the rhythm of life almost stops.

Jesus spoke of the theme of His life, "We must work the works of him who sent me, while it is day; night comes, when no one can work."

There's more to the work of God than singing in choirs. I can't do everything in the work of God, but I can sing. For me, singing brings out the melody in life.

PRAYER: Lord, work with us through the little things of each day to bring us to Your will. Override the static in our lives that we may hear the beauty of Your melody.
                              In Christ,
                              Amen.

Chapter 11

PROUD TO BE A HYPOCRITE

> "But the tax collector, standing far off, would not even lift up his eyes to heaven, but beat his breast, saying, 'God be merciful to me a sinner!' I tell you, this man went down to his house justified rather than the other; for every one who exalts himself will be humbled, but he who humbles himself will be exalted."
>
> LUKE 18:13-14

Wearing a robe bothers me. I recognize the importance of symmetry to the eye. It dresses up the choir and adds order to the worship service. But wearing a robe also makes me feel a bit hypocritical. "A robe," Jack said, laughing at his protruding stomach, "will cover a multitude of sins." That bothers me.

I remember hearing too many people say, "I won't go to church. They're a bunch of hypocrites. I'm no saint but at least I'm no hypocrite." Such judgments against the church disturb me, not because I think they're wrong, but because I know they're right. I am a hypocrite.

When I joined the church, I brought all my human failings with me. I fail to live up to my own goals, much less God's goals for me. But that's why I'm in the church. I need to be here. Someone said,

"The church is not a society for saints, but a hospital for sinners." This is the proper place for those of us who don't measure up.

I'm proud to be a hypocrite. It takes a certain amount of courage. No matter how we condemn hypocrisy, it presupposes an ideal. Anyone can avoid failure by simply not standing for anything, living life on the lowest level. But the shame of life is not in losing the race but in not running at all.

Jesus didn't condemn those who recognized their failings. He forgave them. Maybe to Jesus, a hypocrite was one who professes what he does not believe, rather than someone who fails to live up to what he professes. When we admit our failings and accept the fact that we're unable to live up to God's standards, it makes us stand with the rest of the human race—all the other hypocrites for whom Jesus died.

PRAYER: Lord, give us high ideals and encourage us to reach them. But when we fail, make us at least glad we tried.
In Christ,
Amen.

Chapter 12

SPEAK TO ONE ANOTHER

"... addressing one another in psalms and hymns and spiritual songs, singing and making melody to the Lord with all your heart, always and for everything giving thanks in the name of our Lord Jesus Christ to God the Father."
EPHESIANS 5:19

"They say it would have killed him if he had been sober. You know how kids are nowadays, all they do is party and get drunk and . . ."

I turned it off. I had already heard more than I wanted to. These few minutes before rehearsal offer us an excellent time to visit with one another, to catch up on news and share concerns. Often, however, it turns into a gossip game.

We had all heard about the accident. We're grateful that no one was seriously hurt. What an ordeal for their parents. *If* they were drunk, they need our loving concern even more. They didn't need our idle talk.

Yet who am I to judge gossipers? I gossip, too. I excuse myself by claiming, "It's only human to say things you regret." But when I do it, I hurt others . . . and myself.

I remember sitting with some friends in the parking lot. We had returned from a meeting and someone made a cutting remark about our minister. "Walker thinks he knows everything."

Immediately, I joined in. "Did you know that he hardly ever visits the poorer families in the church?"

For fifteen minutes, we dissected a man we hardly knew and I behaved no differently than the others. A moment later, walking alone to my car, I nearly drowned in guilt. I would have been devastated if Reverend Walker ever heard what I had said about him. Most of it was biased, some of it untrue.

Why did I do it? To look superior? In retrospect, it only made me look childish and unkind. Whatever the reason, I hated myself for doing it.

Two weeks later, our choir sang Jean Berger's anthem, "Speak to one another." The music sounds out a command. As I sang it, I said to myself, "Speak *to* one another, not *about* one another." Of all His creatures, God gave speech and God-consciousness to humans only. He meant for us to use the voice to praise Him, not to hurt others.

PRAYER: Lord, forgive us for our careless use of words. They seem so small but can hurt so much.
>In Christ,
>Amen.

Chapter 13

HELP, THEY ARE CRITICIZING ME!

> "Blessed are you when men revile you and persecute you and utter all kinds of evil against you falsely on my account. Rejoice and be glad, for your reward is great in heaven, for so men persecuted the prophets who were before you."
> MATTHEW 5:11-12

I shouldn't be surprised that they criticize us. The only way to avoid criticism is to do nothing. Rise above the ordinary, and someone finds fault. Heathens accused the early Christians of cannibalism, orgies, and disrupting family life. They even criticized Jesus who lived the most loving and noble life ever lived. Yet they tagged Him with every degrading label they could think of.

But I'm not Jesus and when Earl said, "I don't see why you folks can't sing the kind of songs we like," I was hurt. It was more the tone of his voice or the way he looked than what he actually said.

I snapped back, "We can't please everybody, Earl."

I'm sure he felt the edge on my voice. That's the way it often goes. Jab for jab. I don't think criticism ever works.

Another jab, "I'm just telling you this for your own good," often veils the truth. It really says, "I have an urge to clobber someone and you're it."

Two things we need to remember. First, criticism seldom helps anyone. If you criticize me, I get defensive. Right or wrong has nothing to do with it. I protect my personhood. Criticism would be less destructive if all of us could rise above impulsive defenses and analyze it. "What can I learn from this?" or "What's really bothering my critic?" These kinds of questions turn disapproval into a positive experience.

Second, we never suffer criticism alone. "For so men persecuted the prophets who were before you," calls us to remember that we are of the church. When we compare our little persecution with the suffering of so many of the faithful, we can almost say, "Okay, what's a little criticism?"

But analysis of criticism doesn't take the sting out of it. We know we are in good company, but each of us still struggles when stinging arrows strike us.

We can learn from them. When we know how much criticism hurts, we can determine not to use it again.

PRAYER: Lord, help us to accept criticism constructively. And help us most of all to be less critical of others.
In Christ,
Amen.

Chapter 14

I'M LATE AGAIN

> "Look carefully then how you walk, not as unwise men but as wise, making the most of the time because the days are evil."
> EPHESIANS 5:15-16

"Doggonit," I said outloud. Another red light. I'll be at least ten minutes late.

It seems I spend half my traveling time rushing somewhere to be late. No one should have to live under such pressure. Yet I do and I'm not alone. A friend said, "If I miss the first section of a revolving door, I'm thrown off schedule the rest of the day." I laughed but I moaned a bit, too. I live behind schedule. Even when I plan a time to leave, I seldom leave on time. No wonder I'm late for choir.

It's a personality thing with me. "You have twenty-four hours a day," Ellen told me last week, "just like everybody else. It's a matter of priorities."

I excuse myself by saying how busy I am, but I really know better. A part of me likes the image. I'm afraid if I show up on time I may not look so important. Some call it the "BMB Syndrome – Behold Me Busy." I act as though I owe it to God and the world to be busy.

"I work better under pressure," I have said. That's not true either. I may work harder, but certainly not better.

I would work better if I managed my time better. More accurately, if I managed myself better in the time I have. Unlike weight or talent, God gives each of us an equal amount of time. Our use of it makes the difference.

I slipped into rehearsal ten minutes after it had begun. "You're late," David screamed at the basses. "If you don't anticipate, you'll always be late." He was speaking to the choir about entrances, but he also spoke to me about a life pattern. I am grateful as recognizing it forces me to work toward doing better. Next week I'll be on time.

PRAYER: Lord, keep us from drifting into destructive patterns that cause us to waste time. Help us to seize the opportunities of each day—one at a time.
                            In Christ,
                            Amen.

Chapter 15

SURPRISED BY WORSHIP

> "O come, let us worship and bow down, let us kneel before the Lord, our Maker!"
>
> PSALM 95:6

I worshipped today . . . I mean really worshipped. That doesn't happen with me often. It's mostly a come-and-go affair.

Worship happens to me in split seconds. It may come at the trailing off of the choir's "Amen" or, sometimes I may find myself hearing some phrase over and over in the prayer that I've repeated so many times I hardly listen to it anymore. Sometimes it may be an idea that leaps out from the dry rattle of the sermon, or the architecture, or a symbol. But every now and then I suddenly get the feeling that God really is here. Underneath are the everlasting arms and He knows my name. When that happens, I worship.

This feeling of worship never stays. I always lose it. My mind wanders on to other things and I feel like I've lost God. But for a moment, I worshipped!

That split second of worship becomes the most important moment in my whole week. It gives meaning to the rest of my life. It reminds me that I am related to God and to His people.

Without worship, I become no more than a smart animal. I don't mean that I misbehave. Rather I see life as no more than the sidewalk and newspaper.

So when I worshipped today, I availed myself of the highest privilege of human activity. I grew a bit with God. As always, it caught me by surprise!

PRAYER: Lord, we thank you for meeting us in worship. Help us to recognize our best times.
In Christ,
Amen.

Chapter 16

REMEMBER WHEN?

> "For if they fall, one will lift up his fellow; but woe to him who is alone when he falls and has not another to lift him up."
> ECCLESIASTES 4:10

"Remember the last time we sang this anthem?" Bob asked as David passed out the music.

"You bet I do. The day of the big snow storm when none of the other basses showed up."

"And that was the day . . ." I began, "that George had his heart attack," we said together.

George has never missed choir. We assumed the snow had kept him home. Then after church, they told us. "I understand the next twenty-four hours are crucial," David had said as we sat in shock. Then, without announcement, someone led us in prayer.

Several of us waited and prayed at the hospital all afternoon. The women of the choir took food for a month, and carpooled the kids.

"Yes, I remember the last time we sang this anthem," I said, "and it's good to have George back."

All during rehearsal I reflected on the friendships a choir shares. A sense of belonging, I thought, grows out of what we do and remember together. Expressions of caring, such as "How's the baby?" and "Did Mary get her scholarship?" bind us to one another. Our choir knows everybody by name and misses anyone absent. It's a small enough group for each member to feel important.

Many who simply "join the worship service" but never get involved in a small group in the church often drift out the back door. On the other hand, those of us who belong to the choir seldom have to carry any burden alone.

"I couldn't possibly leave the church," one soprano said, "unless the whole choir went with me. I need them too much."

The teacher in Ecclesiastes affirms the value of partnership. "If they fall, one will lift up his fellow."

Nearly four hundred years later, Paul thanks God for "partnership in the gospel." I, too, feel gratitude for the fellowship I experience in choir.

PRAYER: Lord, give us a loving concern for one another as we work and share together. Bless our fellowship.
　　　　　　　　　　In Christ,
　　　　　　　　　　Amen.

Chapter 17

GRIPES OR GRATITUDE?

> "Not that I complain of want; for I have learned, in whatever state I am, to be content."
> PHILIPPIANS 4:11

"It's not fair to wear robes. I can't put on my Mother's Day corsage," Lillian whined. Last week, she grumbled about being hot during worship. The week before that, her husband caused her to be late. With Lillian, it was always something.

Some people are born pessimists. They constantly see the gloomy side of life, much as expressed in the familiar:

Two men looked out through the same bars;
One sees mud, the other sees stars.
Author unknown.

Unfortunately, most of those "who program themselves negative" feel compelled to air their gripes. Complaining becomes a habit. "We have a right to sound off on our opinion," Jack said, "especially when we feel abused."

Yet Paul writing from prison says, "Do all things without grumbling." Paul had been hounded by a thorn in the flesh; he had suffered shipwrecks, beatings and rejection. Yet he refused to complain.

Grumbling reflects a deep, serious self-centeredness which leaves us feeling alone. It seems innocent, but when we complain it's usually against *someone*. It makes the hearers uncomfortable and takes the joy out of working together. Grumbling not only destroys fellowship, it robs us of energy and enthusiasm and it makes gratitude impossible. When Paul said, "I have learned, in whatever state I am, to be content," he spoke more of his trust in God than his personality. The choice between gratitude and gripes results in either fellowship or loneliness.

A proverb says, "Those who wish to sing always find a song."

PRAYER: Lord, give us the kind of faith in your goodness that frees us from grumbling. Fill us with the joy of serving You together.
                                    In Christ,
                                    Amen.

Chapter 18

INSTANT EVERYTHING

> "But when the king came in to look at the guests, he saw there a man who had no wedding garment; and he said to him, 'Friend, how did you get in here without a wedding garment?'"
> MATTHEW 22:11-12

"Let's warm up," David said. "Both feet on the floor, backs straight and hum on A."

Every rehearsal begins with a warm up. We work at getting ready to sing. Without taking time for preparation, singing proves disastrous. Just as we rehearse to perform, we warm up to rehearse; but most of us don't like vocal exercises. Preparations bore us.

We live in a push button world. Flick a switch and we have instant everything, machine money and complete dinners ready in a minute.

We seem most willing to prepare for the worst in life. We buy insurance in case of disaster, check the oil to keep the car from breaking down, and put up storm windows to keep out the cold. We prepare for rain but give little thought to sunny days.

Yet how much we miss because we are not ready for the good. Some things like education, personal character, and a relationship with God can hardly wait until the last hour.

Jesus said the king rebuked the improperly dressed wedding guest for being too casual. He had not shown respect for a wedding feast.

So what about us? How often do we seek to worship with poor preparation? God does not jump to our beck and call. He is not a servant or mechanic. We prepare ourselves for an experience with Him by showing interest in the things He stands for. We can approach Him with faith and reverence and be ready for a moment with Him when it happens.

We prepare for the things we take seriously.

PRAYER: Lord, we want everything now. Give us the willingness to prepare for better experiences later.
In Christ,
Amen.

Chapter 19

FRIENDLY HABITS

> "And he came to Nazareth, where he had been brought up; and he went to the synagogue, as his custom was, on the sabbath day."
> LUKE 4:16

"Do it again," David said. "We feel rhythm only when the body has it memorized. Then we sing it correctly by habit."

Much of our life depends upon habit. Who can know what sequences of muscle movements we use to tie a shoe, or drive a car? God did us a favor when he made us creatures of habit. LeNelle said, "If I had to stop and think everytime I played a key, soon you'd look for a new organist." Habits have power. We survive by forming good ones.

But habits can makes slaves of us also. Those who bite their nails, or wake up in time to go to work even though it's Saturday, know the control of addiction. Almost anything, good or bad, can become a habit. Do it once and it's easier to do the next time. Someone said, "It would be easier to find a man who has never sinned than to find one who has not committed the same sin twice."

"Sew an art, reap a habit.
Sew a habit and reap a character."

That insight recognizes the importance of a single decision. Everything we do sets up a pattern. Deliberate choices today become second nature tomorrow.

"Sing it right until it becomes a habit," David urged us.

The writer to the Hebrews said, ". . . not neglecting to meet together, as is the habit of some." We have important choices to make.

Belonging to the choir requires us to share at least one good routine with Jesus. It can also be said of us, "As his custom was, he entered the temple to worship."

PRAYER: Lord, help us to cultivate habits that build better character to serve You. Thank You also for the renewal of worship we experience week after week.
In Christ,
Amen.

Chapter 20

DO IT AGAIN

> "An athlete is not crowned unless he competes according to the rules. It is the hardworking farmer who ought to have the first share of the crops."
> II TIMOTHY 2:5-6

"Let's do it again," David said. "The only way to get this right is to work at it. We have to sing it so well that it appears easy to the congregation."

Every bone in me wanted to call it quits. We had been rehearsing for two hours. Many of us felt that we were singing it well enough, but not David. "We must sing our best when we sing for God," he said.

My tired body rebelled but my heart agreed. Greatness is the product of hard work. Many talented artists, athletes and preachers fail because of lack of discipline. Most disciplines, like preparing an anthem, start out easy. We begin exercise and study programs with enthusiasm. Dieters easily lose the first pound. Then temptation shows us attractive, less demanding compromises and we join the large ranks of the mediocre.

"Do it again" reflects only a small part of the requirements of a good choir. Other disciplines include arriving on time, controlling conversation, keeping my body in good physical shape, my mind alert, and controlling my diet to keep me in best voice.

Why do I do it? For the joy of sharing in work well done, or knowing that I live life on a higher plane? Yes. I reap the rewards of feeling like a "good and faithful servant." But even more, I believe in the choir as a part of the total mission of the church.

We are called to change the world. I can't be casual about that.

PRAYER: Lord, Now that we have committed ourselves to a higher cause, help us to show the self-control necessary to do our best. Remind us of your sacrifice when we begin to relax our disciplines.

In Christ,
Amen.

Chapter 21

SURPRISED BY REWARD

> "His master said to him, 'Well done, good and faithful servant; you have been faithful over a little, I will set you over much; enter into the joy of your master'."
> MATTHEW 25:21

"Ed, you have a beautiful voice," she said.

"Oh, I do?" he responded. "Then give all the credit to the Lord. I just sing to praise Him."

I don't know why Ed's piety disturbs me. I guess I don't trust him. I hope I don't serve God to earn some profit, but I confess I find singing in the choir rewarding.

On the way home, I asked my daughter, "Do we serve God hoping for some payoff?"

"I hope not. It sort of reduces God to an accountant. I give Him a dime's worth of service and He awards me a dime's worth of blessing, with profit, of course. I don't like that," she said. "Where does love fit in?"

I agree with my daughter. We relate to God by love, not law. We could give God all we own and still not balance the books. We will always be in debt to Him. His goodness expresses His grace, but never His obligation to us. I wish we could remove reward as motive.

Yet Jesus appealed to rewards in His parables and the Sermon on the Mount. To the faithful servant He said, "Well done, good and faithful servant; you have been faithful over a little, I will set you over much; enter into the joy of your master." Good works are better than bad works in God's eyes and He does not respond to them in the same way. Someone said, "Remove rewards and apathy has the last word."

While I seek to serve God because I love Him, at the same time I am aware that my faithfulness brings an inner satisfaction. Sometimes I am rewarded with more work to do, but always the reward catches me by surprise. I never feel deserving of it. God gives it out of His grace and that's the greatest prize of all.

Yes, I do find singing in the choir rewarding.

PRAYER: Lord, help us to serve because we love you. And when you reward us, fill us with surprised gratitude.
                In Christ,
                Amen.

Chapter 22

FAITH, REGARDLESS

> "Then Job arose, and rent his robe, and shaved his head, and fell upon the ground, and worshipped."
> JOB 1:20

As we sang our closing hymn, "O Love That Wilt Not Let Me Go," I thought about it. I enjoyed the music but most of all, I appreciated its message. God does hold on to us.

Then I looked over and saw the Nelsons as they sang. Immediately I scanned the congregation to find Gene, their retarded son. I couldn't hear him but I knew that in his off-pitch voice he sang it, too. Seeing them, I realized life's easy for me. The worst I've suffered is a toothache. How can the Nelsons affirm the love of God with the anguish they bear?

Are they, like Job, reaching out to God because they have no other place to turn? When life deals harshly with us we can withdraw into bitterness and self-pity, or we can reach out to God, even if we feel we are reaching in the dark. Some even claim to find their closest touch with God from the bottom of the pit.

Maybe they sang to God out of gratitude. "We are so thankful that our other children are normal," Lehman Nelson once said, "So many families have more than one child afflicted. We thank God for every accomplishment Gene makes." Often when we suffer, we focus on the pain and forget the good. Someone pointed out that we are prone to play most on the frayed string.

Not so the Nelsons. They trust God, regardless. I'm sure they don't understand all that has happened to them but they continue to praise God.

As we continued to sing, I also thought of George Matheson, a young man with a bright future. The bottom dropped out for him, too. He became completely blind and his fiancee deserted him. But in faith, he plowed on, becoming probably the greatest preacher in Scotland. After years of reaching out in faith and gratitude, he wrote:

> "O Love, that wilt not let me go,
> I rest my weary soul in thee,
> I give thee back the life I owe,
> that in thine ocean depths its flow
> May richer, fuller be."

PRAYER: Lord, when we come to the place where life caves in, give us faith.

In Christ,
Amen.

Chapter 23

THE HOPE OF DEATH

> "Death is swallowed up in victory. O death, where is thy victory? O death, where is thy sting?' The sting of death is sin, and the power of sin is the law. But thanks be to God, who gives us the victory through our Lord Jesus Christ."
> I CORINTHIANS 15:54b-57

Ruby died. We expected it.

For six months she fought a losing battle against cancer. After each visit, members of the choir reported her growing weakness. We should have been prepared. But suddenly realizing that her empty chair would never be filled again shocked us.

Why? I wondered. Ruby, of all people.

She glowed with love, faith and optimism. She put peanuts on her ice cream and bragged about her children. If anyone deserved to live, Ruby did.

The rest of us go on. We rehearse and sing week after week. Then, suddenly someone dies and we no longer live on the surface. All life is not melodious.

"Death is swallowed up in victory." How contrary! In our experience, every victory is swallowed up in death. Even the quality life of a Ruby . . . dies.

We cannot deny the fact of death. The meaning of death is another matter. "In Christ shall all be made alive," said Paul. And again, "To die is gain."

The scriptures promise that death is the edge of life, not the end of it. Not much description of what that life is like, it's described only in terms of relationships. We shall be with Christ. Nothing more could be added.

But how do we know? As always with the things of God, it's a matter of faith. But it's either that God has an eternal and glorious plan for Ruby and us, or neither life nor death has any meaning.

There can be no meaning in the here and now unless there's hope for the there and then.

PRAYER: Lord, we cry in death for the pain it inflicts. Yet we also rejoice in the hope it promises.
In Christ,
Amen.

Chapter 24

BECKY QUIT

> "I have fought the good fight, I have finished the race, I have kept the faith."
> II TIMOTHY 4:7

Becky no longer sings with us. She quit!

I haven't quit but I thought about it a thousand times. I have all kinds of reasons for quitting. To keep on displays nothing newsworthy. To do again what I did last week, and the week before that. What's the big deal?

My weekly loyalty may seem ordinary but we build a great choir on those who say, "I will not quit." Our faithfulness may not be spectacular but it's essential for the church.

Some say the church suffers most not from some terrible enemy but from its leaders giving up. I have no criticism of tennis or home repairs unless these good things replace better things. To substitute less for the best constantly tempts us. Unless we set priorities, the things that matter the most often fall to the mercy of things that matter the least.

Many start who never finish. Staying power makes the difference. When I am tempted to quit, I think of two things.

First, I realize how little I sacrifice for Christ. I sing in the choir, have given a tithe for years, and once I even taught an adult class. But fighting a good fight and keeping the faith against adversaries hardly qualifies me as a beginner, much less as one ready to quit.

Then I also remember that God is faithful to me to the end. He must have a dozen reasons to give up on me, but even the cross did not turn Him back.

I regret Becky's quitting but her absence makes me reaffirm my own steadfastness. I believe in the importance of my simple service to the choir. I will not quit!

PRAYER: Lord, help us when we are tempted to quit to remember the importance of what we do. Enable us to respond to your faithfulness to us with faithfulness to you.

In Christ,
Amen.

Chapter 25

INTERRUPTED SCHEDULES

> "Now Peter and John were going up to the temple at the hour of prayer, the ninth hour. And a man lame from birth was being carried, whom they laid daily at that gate of the temple which is called Beautiful to ask alms of those who entered the temple. Seeing Peter and John about to go into the temple, he asked for alms."
>
> ACTS 3:1-3

Running late and out of breath, I rushed up the steps to the sanctuary. Rehearsal started ten minutes ago. I reached for the door. Then I saw him.

He looked a hundred years old and it must have been a month since he had combed his hair, brushed his teeth or had a bath. Immediately I knew what he wanted, but he still frightened me.

"Mister, I need some help. I ain't had nothing to eat all day and the doctor said I need an operation and my daughter went and..."

I didn't hear the rest of it. I had heard it before. He was just a bum. Why did he stop me now when I'm running late? "Okay," I said handing him five dollars. "I hope things go better for you tomorrow."

"But mister, the last bus done run and I ain't got no way now to get back down town. You couldn't give me a lift, could ya'?"

Ten minutes later, driving back to the church somewhat relieved to be rid of him, I struggled with mixed feelings. I don't always handle interruptions well, and no matter how carefully I plan, I get constantly interrupted. Some of them are big, like financial reversals and accidents. Others are more permanent, like transfers or death. No one escapes interruptions, but we can learn to make the best of them.

Some interruptions turn out to be good. Jesus honored every opportunity to help another person. He healed the sick and fed the hungry. Peter and John sacrificed prayer time to give what they had to the lame man. Most interruptions contain a hidden opportunity.

By keeping an eye on my larger goal of serving Christ, I can belong to the beggar and to the choir. I missed most of the rehearsal, but I was on target for the message the choir sings.

PRAYER: Lord, interrupt our schedules when we get so busy telling the faith that we fail to live it.
       In Christ,
       Amen.

Chapter 26

ONLY ONE EXPRESSION

> "There is one body and one spirit, just as you were called to the one hope that belongs to your call, one Lord, one faith, one baptism, one God and Father of us all, who is above all and through all and in all."
> EPHESIANS 4:4-6

"Thursday we rehearse with the choir at St. Johns," David said. "Time for another joint service."

I like combining our choirs for special occasions. It announces that both churches really are the same body even though we worship in different buildings. We do other things together. Our kids go to the same schools, we shop in the same stores and vote for the same politicians. It seems we share everything in our community but our faith.

We believe in one Christ and profess one church. Yet Christians are divided 250 ways. Society seems more together than the church.

I dislike the "we only" preachers. I heard one last week on the radio. He insisted at the top of his voice that his followers were the only true disciples. "Only a few," he kept repeating. Had he announced that few would be saved, but unfortunately he was not one of them, I would have listened to him much longer. But he insisted that he, himself, represented the center of the fold.

My church affirms a more universal appreciation for the Body of Christ. I'm pleased to recognize the value of other Christian expressions. As Paul said, some are feet, others hands, or eyes; many gifts, one body.

I don't even like to think of our church as a branch of the same tree. This implies that we are separate from the other branches. Rather I think of our church as an expression. We make one sound in God's symphony. We may be only the piccolo, but our part mixes with all the others to make up the church.

PRAYER: Lord, make us a more authentic expression of the church as we claim our oneness.
In Christ,
Amen.

Chapter 27

REACTION TO GRACE

> "What shall I render to the Lord for all his bounty to me? I will lift up the cup of salvation and call on the name of the Lord."
> PSALM 116:12-13

Today we celebrate the Lord's Supper. I always feel uneasy on Communion Sundays. I feel so unworthy.

"This is my body broken for you." I don't deserve that kind of love. I try hard to earn the right. If God would be willing for me to pay for even a part of it, I wouldn't feel so . . . dependent. I live in a culture that says you only get what you pay for. To accept God's love totally unearned is a big step for me. I'd rather at least partially deserve it.

Yet I remember hearing Reverend Walker say, "You cannot move God to love you. He loves out of His own heart, never because we merit it." If I understand Him, to recognize my unworthiness is the closest to worthy I can become.

Then do we drag ourselves to the Lord's Table beating our breasts? No, we come celebrating His love for us with gratitude. "What shall I render to the Lord for all his bounty to me? I will lift up the cup of salvation and call on the name of the Lord," said the Psalmist. God gives out of His love; we receive out of our gratitude. This action-reaction of the Lord's Supper keeps bringing us back to the basic theme of the Christian faith. No wonder Jesus commanded that we eat and drink it often in remembrance of Him. Otherwise, we may forget and think the action is ours and the reaction God's . . . or that He responds to our deeds.

The Lord's Supper, like the A-440, brings us back to the standard pitch. The true note of the gospel is grace.

PRAYER: Lord, as we partake of this supper, call us again to remember the grace of Your love. Give us faith to receive it in gratitude, lest we wobble off key.
       In Christ,
       Amen.

Chapter 28

DOING WHAT I CAN

> ". . . to one he gave five talents, to another two, to another one, to each according to his ability. Then he went away."
> MATTHEW 25:15

"We need Sunday school teachers," Reverend Walker announced. "God calls you into service."

My kids are in Sunday school but I have no talent for teaching. Ted sings in the choir but he also teaches an adult class. He is one of those five-talent guys. I have one talent. I can sing.

God did not create us all equal. Some, for no apparent reason, get five talents; others four, and most of us only one or two. The person with five has the edge, for the gap between the many and lesser talents continues to widen. That's the way life is.

No wonder many one-talented people grow cynical. The deck is stacked against them, they complain, but that's no excuse. We can either shut down in self-pity or we can use the one talent we have for God's glory.

I don't teach but I can do my share. All members of the choir can't sing solos but we each have a part to carry. I can't be anyone else and I'd look like a fool to try. God expects me to do the best I can with my limited talent. I have only one but I'm learning to appreciate it. The excitement of belonging to the one talent army comes from knowing that footsoldiers, not generals, win battles. The church depends upon the masses of one-talented lay people each carrying a bit of the load. The miracle of a choir augments the numerous tones of mediocre voices into the harmony of a symphony.

Few of us possess unusual talents. God simply calls each of us to use what He gives us in service to Him.

PRAYER: Lord, we thank you for every gift. Help us to use it for you.
In Christ,
Amen.

Chapter 29

DEALING WITH ANGER

> "Be not quick to anger, for anger lodges in the bosom of fools."
> ECCLESIASTES 7:9

When I reached for my robe, it was gone. "Why can't people be more careful?" I said out loud. I don't know why it angered me so but I was peeved and everyone knew it.

Later, the memory of my short fuse embarrassed me.

Why had I let it happen? To attract attention or to intimidate others? For whatever reason, it immobilized me. Unless I learn to handle rage better, it could destroy me. Uncontrolled anger causes more than ulcers. I believe it serves no good purpose.

Even though I direct anger toward others, the only person I can ever really change is me. When Ellen irritates me, she may change in response to my reaction, but she may not. If I alter my behavior only to manipulate her, it never works. My anger mostly affects me.

In fact, most of my wrath grows out of what's going on within me and not from external happenings. Last month at the end of a hard day, I went home. Just as I walked through the kitchen, our eight-year-old son dropped the ice tray. Bang! Ice scattered all over the floor.

"Jim, you always drop the ice tray," I snapped and walked out.

Ten minutes later, I had forgotten the entire incident when Jim tiptoed into the room. Sniffling and wiping tears from his cheek, he whimpered, "Daddy . . . Daddy, that's the first time I ever dropped the ice tray."

Suddenly I realized he had not caused my rage. I had brought it home with me. Jim had simply become a means of my unloading it.

I could have chosen a better way to handle anger. When I become aware of anger, I need to share it with a friend. By admitting my emotions to another, I can choose to disarm their destructive forces. Or even better, I can laugh at it. When I consider the importance of having my robe missing compared to the colossal problems of the world, my irritation is ludicrous. I can choose to laugh at it and be happy, or become angry and feel sick.

PRAYER: Lord, bless us with the joy of being meek, lest we destroy ourselves with anger.
          In Christ,
          Amen.

Chapter 30

THE RISK OF NOT GIVING

> "The point is this: he who sows sparingly will also reap sparingly and he who sows bountifully will also reap bountifully. Each one must do as he has made up his mind, not reluctantly or under compulsion, for God loves a cheerful giver."
> II CORINTHIANS 9:6-7

They never pass the offering plate to the choir. That makes it easy for me not to give. I can't get to my wallet because of the robe.

Those who sit in the pew have a nudge of conscience when they put nothing in the plate. But me? My giving or not goes unnoticed. I have to make a special effort to pay a pledge.

Some of us feel we do our share by singing in the choir. We give our time and talent and can let others pay the bills. But I don't give to meet the needs of the church. I give to express my faith. If giving were motivated by the church's budget, then we could all join a rich church and be Christians for free. Neither do I give because of what I can afford. I give because of what I *believe*, not because of what I *have*. I need to give.

One way I know to combat the feeling that everything of value can be bought and sold is to give away some money. No matter whether I give two dollars or two hundred, as soon as I give it, I declare that I seek meaning in ways not commercial. Generosity is the way I have to combat materialism.

I also give to feel a sense of belonging. Those who don't give seldom call on the pastor in time of trouble. They don't participate in church programs or share in the dreams of the congregation. But when I give, I become a part of all the church does. I belong!

Give until it hurts? No, that's not enough. I give until it feels good. It takes a little more effort to give my money since I sing in the choir. I have to go out of my way to give, but it's worth it.

PRAYER: Lord, show us the excitement of giving time, talent, and money that we may find the things we value most.
In Christ,
Amen.

Chapter 31

FALLING OUT OF EDEN

> "... and be renewed in the
> spirit of your minds..."
> EPHESIANS 4:23

"I don't see how we can rehearse tonight," Margie said. "We're all too upset."

"About what?" I asked, realizing that something had happened.

"George and Betty. They're splitting up. I understand he has already moved out . . . they are getting a divorce."

I tried to remain detached but it struck me like a slap in the face. Betty had sung in the choir for ten years. She and George participated in everything. The entire congregation loved them both. What happened? And what happened to the adage, "The family that prays together stays together?" Most of all, how do we help them now?

"I don't care how bad things seemed, as Christians they took a vow to stick it out." Margie expressed her anger by appealing to the law. "Divorce is a sin and I'll never feel right about them again."

Some say the worst reconciliation is better than the best divorce, but I don't know. Marriages may be made in heaven, but they must be lived out here among sinful people. God's laws are perfect, but those of us who try to live them are not. We fail in many ways.

Certainly divorce is a sin. It breaks God's will for us. He didn't plan for marriages to dissolve. One man, one woman for life is an ideal, but not a law. God opposes divorce not to uphold a law but because in divorce people get hurt.

Then what about Betty?

We must keep this "sin" in proper prospective. What we say of divorce must be said of other failings. We act unjustly to single out divorce as something unique. I think we should also remember that God forgives. Jesus always showed more interest in what a person could become than in what a person had been. We can recognize that Betty will now experience the loneliest time of her life. We, as a choir, can become an extended family to her. We can help fill the emptiness.

PRAYER: Lord, our humanness shocks us. Help us to not cover up our fear of failure by becoming judgmental but rather make us proclaimers of forgiveness.
In Christ,
Amen.

Chapter 32

FEELING FORGIVEN

> "And the son said to him, 'Father, I have sinned against heaven and before you; I am no longer worthy to be called your son.' But the father said to his servants, 'Bring quickly the best robe and put it on him; and put a ring on his hand and shoes on his feet; and bring the fatted calf and kill it, and let us eat and make merry; for this my son was dead and is alive again; he was lost, and is found.' And they began to make merry."
>
> LUKE 15:21-24

I needed, deserved, planned, paid for and appreciated this vacation . . . until this morning. Suddenly, I feel guilty. It's Sunday and I'm not in choir.

Guilt is my quickest emotion! It doesn't take much to get it going. Almost anything sexual or relating to anger will do it. If I even forget to take out the trash, my guilt machine goes into production.

Yet in my head I know guilt's a futile emotion. Sometimes the feelings of guilt have no basis in real fact. To examine my wrongs and learn from them would be helpful. However, I usually deal with guilt in destructive ways. I throw the book at myself and wallow in self-blame. "If I feel guilty enough, it seems I should be exonerated," I once said. But for whatever reason, I seek to combat guilt by self-condemnation and it never works.

On the other hand, I often deal with guilt by blaming others. I find someone else responsible for making me late or dishonest. Adam blamed Eve and Eve blamed the devil, but Adam's guilt remained and mine does, too.

Psychiatrists say my unresolved guilt may cause everything from headaches to accidents, but I still cling to my self-indictments like prized possessions. I could deal better with guilt by sharing it. Find someone I can trust and simply say, "This is who I am. I don't like it, but this is what I've done." Someone knowing and caring for me disarms my guilt.

Also, important in dealing with my guilt involves how I perceive God. Is He a Father or a Judge? The father forgave the prodigal and welcomed him home. I believe a father is like that even when He is God.

PRAYER: Lord, help us to trust in your forgiveness so much that we may even be able to forgive ourselves.
In Christ,
Amen.

Chapter 33

WORRY TRAP

> "And which of you by being anxious can add one cubit to his span of life?"
> MATTHEW 6:27

We sing, "He's got the whole world in his hands," yet I jump everytime the phone rings.

Our twenty-year-old son, Tom, was not home when I left for rehearsal. We expected him over two hours ago. He drives all day to get home but it's unlike him to be late.

"No ice on bridges yet," the radio said, "but . . ." I can't help but worry.

Part of me feels that if I show a proper amount of worry, it serves as prayer. God will notice my concern and share it. I know better. I'm not buying God's protection.

Worry has no redemptive qualities. It spoils living, destroys health and denies faith. It does no good. Jesus said, "Which of you by being anxious can add one cubit to his span of life?"

Yet, I worry, until the phone rings and I hear that my son is home safe. I live with a contradiction. I know God holds the whole world in His hands, but at the same time, some sons don't get home.

If I could do anything to insure Tom's safety, I would. Action is the best way to deal with worry, but here I am forced to accept my human limitations.

I like the famous serenity prayer which goes:

"God give me the courage to change the things I can change;
The patience to accept the things I cannot change,

And the wisdom to know the difference."
But I would add to it,
"And the faith to know your presence with me through it all."
My worry makes the future no better and the present less effective. But when my son arrives I always look to God with intense gratitude and feel His presence.

PRAYER: O Lord, Give us the faith and wisdom to release our worry.
In Christ,
Amen.

Chapter 34

GOD WITHIN

> "For where two or three are gathered in my name, there am I in the midst of them."
> MATTHEW 18:20

"I hate sitting up here in front of all these people," Jack whispered during the prelude. "I wish our choir were in the balcony."

"You've got to be kidding," I said. "I hate singing to the back of heads."

"At least you could nap during the sermon," he joked.

"You do that anyhow!"

"Seriously," he said, "when I stand and face the congregation, it feels like a performance for the people rather than worship of God."

Throughout the rest of the service, I struggled with Jack's concern. Do we sing for God or the congregation?

Of course we sing to God. We lift our praise to Him as an offering of worship. John Calvin taught that the choir's job is to respond to the proclaimed Word. Therefore he seated them in the back of the room. But respond is not all we do.

I believe the choir also *proclaims* the Word and should be up in front of the people. We lead the congregation in prayer. We also teach.

God speaks through us. Eye contact, facial expressions, and how we look is as relevant as how we sound.

The only thing irrelevant is the old argument of whether we sing to God or His people. Of course we sing to the Lord, but not a God up there someplace. We sing to God dwelling among His people. We may never understand but in worship we experience Him. Our value in singing is to enable us all, by emotions, insights, and aesthetics to become more aware of God within us.

PRAYER: O Lord, free us from the fear of performance that we may be open to express your presence. We believe you speak through us, so help us to sing with all our being.
In Christ,
Amen.

Chapter 35

OUR VISUAL MESSAGE

> "But when the king came in to look at the guests, he saw there a man who had no wedding garment; and he said to him, 'Friend, how did you get in here without a wedding garment?' And he was speechless."
> MATTHEW 22:11-12

"It sure is hot," Jack whispered to me. "Especially in these robes. I don't see why we have to wear them."

"I like them," I replied.

"Too much trouble and expense," he said. "What are we trying to hide?"

Jack's right about the cost involved. Buying robes for each choir, cleaning and storing them is expensive and they can be hot! But I like what a robe represents.

Choir robes, like uniforms, cover our differences in dress. We don't consider the worship service as a fashion show, yet the contrast in dress among choir members could be distracting or even ludicrous. Choir robes also announce to me and other worshippers that this is a special occasion. We gather to worship God and a special dress declares more than business as usual.

Even more the uniformity of our dress shows visually what we proclaim vocally. We are one. God covers us in a common grace and we express a kindred response. We worship as a family. The symmetry of choir robes represents the message of our kinship to one another as Christians and our respect for the One we worship.

Jesus tells of the king who rebuked the disrespectful guest for being improperly dressed. In the same way, something inside me feels uncomfortable when I am too casual in worship. I don't want to put on a show. God loves *me*, not my clothes, but it's a matter of respect that I appear before Him dressed for the occasion.

In spite of the trouble and expense, I sing better when robed.

PRAYER: O Lord, we come to worship with many moods and expressions. Yet we are one in our need to praise You. Help us in every way we can to feel our unity.
                In Christ,
                Amen.

Chapter 36

GIVE ME PATIENCE, NOW

> "Love is patient and kind; love is not jealous or boastful; . . ."
> I CORINTHIANS 13:4

"I hate combined choir rehearsals," Bob said. "Dave has explained that same procedure to the Junior Choir at least four times."

In the meantime we adults stood in our places and waited for the children to get it right. "Patience, Bob," I said.

"Humpf. It's harder for me to wait than to work."

I know how he feels. We live in a culture that holds little admiration for patience. We rush forward and get things done. Our world wants action!

Yet Paul, in describing love, starts with patience. Without it, love cannot last. Sooner or later relationships are put to a test. A child loses his place, a wife comes in late, or the mail gets lost. I don't need patience when everything unfolds my way. I get irritated when others don't act, think, or talk the way I want them to. My impatience demands that they all agree with me.

How naive! Only a person who has never failed has a right to be impatient. I don't even live up to my own standards, much less God's. Is my impatience a cover-up? Am I trying to present myself as "the righteous one" whom God is fortunate to have in His church? The truth is I know God has expended an endless amount of patience on me. In His eyes, I'm a child, too.

So I listen as David explains it one more time. He allows children to behave like children and doesn't require them to be who they are not.

I thank God, whose day is like a thousand years, for allowing me time to grow up and learn patience.

PRAYER: O Lord, we thank You that when You say "I'll love you forever," that You mean "I'll be patient with you forever."
In Christ,
Amen.

Chapter 37

GOD CALLS IN A WHISPER

> "Then the Lord called 'Samuel! Samuel!' and he said, 'Here am I!' and ran to Eli, and said, 'Here I am, for you called me.' But he said, 'I did not call; lie down again.' So he went and lay down."
>
> I SAMUEL 3:4-5

I listened to the sermon.

Reverend Walker said, "And God calls you just as loudly and clearly as He called the prophets and disciples." I heard Walker up to that point, but God's calls to me are seldom loud or clear.

When God calls me, I thought, it's always in a whisper. He never seems to call me loud enough for anyone else to hear. I yearn for some confirmation of God's will for my life. Without it I respond with a measure of reservation. "Is this really God's call?"

I wonder about others, especially Paul. He, alone, heard the call of Christ for himself. The others with him only saw a light and heard thunder. Years later, after shipwreck, persecution and stonings in prison, I wonder if Paul felt any reservation. Did he ask, "Was it really Christ I saw, or was it just a great light?"

Not only does God call softly, His call can always sound like something else, something natural. Three times Samuel thought the call of God was the voice of Eli. God's call can usually be explained away.

I believe God does call me, but if I am to hear it, I must lean into it. He could speak in a voice as he did to Samuel and Paul, but most often He communicates with me through a flower's beauty or a storm or even an anthem. And I am learning to hear Him when I listen.

PRAYER: O Lord, make us open to Your call. Speak to us in a still, small voice and give us faith to listen.
In Christ,
Amen.

Chapter 38

SAM'S GOAL IS DEATH

> "I consider that the sufferings of this present time are not worth comparing with the glory that is to be revealed to us."
> ROMANS 8:18

Poor Sam . . . stricken with Multiple Sclerosis six years ago. No remission. He can hardly walk the three steps to the bass section even with the help of two friends and a walker. Sam has been in and out of the hospital more than a hundred times in the past three years. Doctors offer no good news. He feels constant pain, yet about once a month, Sam makes it to choir.

"How do you cope with it?" I once asked him.

"At first, I denied that I had MS," he replied. "Then I felt hostile toward God . . . and toward all healthy people. But now I'm resigned to it."

He cried, and I put my arms around his shoulders.

"I don't want to die," he said, "but that's all that's left." The anguish on his face shocked me. I had nothing to say. I held his hand.

After a few moments he said, "Thanks."

Later, I asked, "Why?" feeling a bit of anger. People testify to finding convenient parking places because they prayed. Others claim immediate relief from toothaches after prayer. Why doesn't God answer all the prayers offered for Sam?

Life asks questions that can't be answered. Jesus made no attempt to sermonize on the problem of suffering. His disciples asked if the man was born blind because of his sins or his parents'? Jesus said, "Neither but this happened that God might be glorified." Of course blindness does not glorify God but how we treat those who suffer does. So it is with Sam.

I have no answers for him or myself, but I honor his feeling. I listen to him and sometimes I can support his uncontrolled body and unstable emotions.

"I'm tired of this life," he said. "I wish the end would come."

For Sam, the end has become a goal, not a termination. I think that's what Paul had in mind when he said, "I consider that the sufferings of this present time are not worth comparing with the glory that is to be revealed to us."

PRAYER: O Lord, we would like to turn away from suffering and death. But it always confronts us. Use it to increase our faith in those glorious things not yet seen.
                    In Christ,
                    Amen.

Chapter 39

I HATE TO SAY "I'M SORRY"

> "And a second is like it, You shall love your neighbor as yourself."
> MATTHEW 22:39

"I'll tell you why Marvin's not here," I announced to the others with authority, "He's probably out working his second job. I've never known anyone so eager to make money. His greed has become more important to him than his church." No one responded. Then I heard it behind me. The door slammed.

"Was that . . .?"

"Yes, it was Marvin," one of the men said, "and I'm afraid he heard what you said."

A nauseous ache grabbed me. Why had I been so stupid? Oh, how I wish I could undo what I had said. The others continued to talk but I felt sick.

As soon as the meeting was over, I drove to Marvin's house. What else could I do? It was a hard trip for I knew I had been wrong. My unkind words had deeply hurt a friend. I prayed that he would accept my apology.

Later that night, I admitted the hardest two words I have ever said are "I'm sorry," but I had to say them.

Saying "I'm sorry" was the only way Marvin could ever let me back into his life. Also, admitting my wrong was the only way I could respect myself. Not only was I wrong to say what I did about Marvin, I was wrong in what I said. I had no knowledge of why he had to take a second job.

Later, before going to sleep, I made myself a promise. From now on I will try to be less concerned with *what* my neighbor does and more concerned with *why* he does it. I give myself that benefit. I could learn to give others the same. When I fail, I always temper it with why, but too often when another fails, all I see is the failure.

As much as I hate to say "I'm sorry," I had better learn in this way also to love my neighbor as myself.

PRAYER: O Lord, give my the courage to say "I'm sorry" when I hurt a friend, and make me more careful with my words.
　　　　　　　　　　　　In Christ,
　　　　　　　　　　　　Amen.

Chapter 40

GOD, SHE MUST BE LONELY

> "The hour is coming, indeed it has come, when you will be scattered, every man to his home, and will leave me alone; yet I am not alone, for the Father is with me."
>
> JOHN 16:32

"How are you?" he greeted me.
"Okay, I guess. My family's been gone for ten days and I'm lonely. I don't like batching it."

Later at rehearsal I looked over at Mimi. She lives alone all the time. Her husband is dead, her children grown and gone.

I remember last year when Mimi shared with us photographs of her family. "Sometimes I talk to my pictures," she had said, "but they never talk back." I knew then how lonely she must be.

What a ministry this choir offers to people like Mimi. Fellowship more than anything else arrests loneliness. At least Mimi can share problems here with friends and know she is missed when absent. We can't change her circumstances, but we can be with her. Just to have a place to go and something to do is not enough. She also needs to know that we care.

Jesus asked for His disciples to be with Him, "He took with Him Peter and James and John and began to be greatly distressed and troubled." They could not lift his cup and He knew it, but their presence comforted Him.

Then they fell asleep. We do what we can to offer caring support to one another, but eventually Mimi, Jesus, and I have only God to comfort us. In the last hour Jesus said, "Yet I am not alone, for the Father is with me. I have said this to you, that in me you may have peace."

Next Sunday when we sing "O Love, That Wilt Not Let Me Go," I will feel a new appreciation for that hymn, and I will be grateful.

PRAYER: O Lord, make those of us in this choir sensitive to the loneliness of one another and help us to feel Your presence.

                                          In Christ,
                                          Amen.

Chapter 41

THOSE WHO HOLD ME

> "No temptation has overtaken you that is not common to man. God is faithful, and he will not let you be tempted beyond your strength, but with the temptation will also provide the way of escape, that you may be able to endure it."
>
> I CORINTHIANS 10:13

"None of us escapes temptation," Reverend Walker said. At first I thought he's not talking about me, at least not to the me that others see. Yet within my private self, I knew he spoke the truth. Temptations come to me regularly, desserts, status symbols, and beautiful women. These among other things attract me daily. Only a fool could deny being tempted.

I don't know why we pretend to be above enticement, especially those of us in the church. Jesus was tempted. The Bible frequently warns us to be on guard. We all live vulnerable lives, especially when we try to set ourselves above allurement.

How much easier it would be for me if I could share the truth of my temptations with an understanding friend. "Hey, George," I need to say, "I don't like what I'm feeling inside and I need you to help me fight against it."

I seldom feel free to admit my weaknesses to people. Certainly in close Christian fellowship like a choir, I can tell my struggles, and because they love me, and support me when temptation strikes, I can trust them. Their love makes me feel as though giant arms enfold me.

The church has always held me. As a child, I sang an old hymn which still speaks a truth for me.

> I would be true,
> For there are those who trust me;
> I would be pure,
> For there are those who care.

Others do care, and when I yield to temptation, they are hurt too. As part of the choir, I live in a fellowship of those who trust me. Some even look up to me as an example. More than anything else their love for me and mine for them guides me through temptation.

However, my greatest resource and that which holds me the closest is Christ's love for me. I don't have to be fretful about temptation for He assures me that even if I do stumble, He still loves me. I can't ultimately fail because Christ holds me. How do I know that? When I experience the fellowship and concern of fellow choir members, I feel Him holding me through them.

PRAYER: O Lord, "Lead us not into temptation," we pray. Make our choir into the kind of supportive fellowship that holds us all.
In Christ,
Amen.

Chapter 42

EMOTIONAL FREEDOM

> "Is anyone among you suffering? Let him pray. Is any cheerful? Let him sing praise."
> JAMES 5:13

Emotions fill my entire body when I sing "Behold What Manner of Love." I fight back tears. Others do too, because for some reason crying in church does not seem proper. I wonder why?

Anytime we become aware of the presence of God, we experience emotion. I'm glad that I feel such things as joy, hope and even sadness. My heart is not made of wood. I often cry and laugh.

Yet some worship leaders discredit emotions. "Nothing more than a sentimental substitute for a real experience with God," they say. They fear some try to create emotional experiences, especially with music, as proof of God's presence. Often such gimmicks are divorced from reason and reality.

Are emotion and reason incompatible? Worship is exciting and often too deep for logic. The sensation of God moves beyond theology and becomes doxology.

Yet the thrill of elevated emotion risks a pitfall. Emotions are fickle and can change without my control. The mysterious mood that lifts me to ecstacy can suddenly plunge me into irrational despair. "I know I should behave differently but I can't do it," someone says who lives by emotional swings. At the same time, depressed emotions sap my energies. Sometimes I even feel like quitting.

So I can't live merely by the way I feel. I have made a decision. I will seek to direct my life according to my *values* and not exclusively by my feelings. I remain loyal and committed to my church, job, home, and responsibilities because I value them, not because I always feel like sustaining them.

I have learned that emotions never remain constant. Nor do they continue to move in the same direction. No matter how high I feel, sooner or later the letdown comes. Likewise, no matter how low I sink, eventually the feeling level rises.

I am an emotional person. In this choir I have opportunity to express my entire catalogue of feelings, but I'm glad for the values that sustain me.

PRAYER: O Lord, we thank You for all the feelings of life, and we thank You for the bounds that set us free.
 In Christ,
 Amen.

Chapter 43

WHEN DEPRESSION COMES

"But he himself went a day's journey into the wilderness, and came and sat down under a broom tree; and he asked that he might die, saying, 'It is enough; now, O Lord, take away my life; for I am no better than my fathers.' And he lay down and slept under a broom tree; and behold, an angel touched him, and said to him, 'Arise and eat.' And he looked, and behold there was at his head a cake baked on hot stones and a jar of water. And he ate and drank, and lay down again."

I KINGS 19:4-6

"The cantata was really great last night, didn't you think?" Bob asked.

"Yeah, I guess."

"Well, you certainly don't sound too enthused. What's the matter?" he asked.

"Oh, I don't know. Guess I'm a little down."

"That's not like you, my friend. If I can do anything to help . . ."

With that, Bob left me alone.

I often feel a letdown after some successful high. Realizing that fact helps me identify with the prophet, Elijah. He had just turned back the forces of Baal when suddenly he lacked the resources to cope. "It is enough; now, O Lord, take away my life." After a victory, many of us are often most vulnerable.

Elijah had worked day and night and he was exhausted. I have also learned that when I run too hard for too long, my fatigue leads to depression.

I don't think anyone knows what brings sadness on, or what causes it to go away, but sooner or later, depression affects us all. Great men such as Martin Luther and Winston Churchill wrote of their "black days." The scriptures record that even "Jesus wept."

Life isn't always cheery. Sometimes I fear Christians feel we must be happy and chipper all the time or we let God down. Yet what hypocrisy to paste on smiles for appearance's sake. Others see through it. Worse still, unless we admit being downcast, it's difficult to work through it.

I think I understand my depression. For many it is related to grief or guilt. But my experience parallels that of Elijah. A heavy heart usually attacks at two times, after a victory or when I'm tired.

But in the same way that sadness slips up on my blindside, I am equally surprised when it subsides. Then I look back on my somber moods, and realize that, like Elijah, I have experienced a closeness to God while in it.

PRAYER: O Lord, help us to trust Your love and the support of friends when we feel depressed. And give us strength to hold on until it's over.

In Christ,
Amen.

Chapter 44

I NEED YOU TO LISTEN

> "But the woman, knowing what had been done to her, came in fear and trembling and fell down before him, and told him the whole truth."
>
> MARK 5:33

". . . and I need to know now if anyone cannot sing on that night," David said.

Suddenly the room grew quiet. David waited for a response and I realized that I hadn't heard a word he said. I had not been listening.

No wonder I miss so much. Listening is my hardest discipline. Often I don't hear what people say to me because I tune them out in order to think through my reply. I want so much to impress with my answer that I pay little attention to the question.

I believe one of our most desperate needs is to have someone listen to us. To tell our story is more therapeutic than any drug.

Someone said, "A pretty girl is one I notice. A charming girl is one who notices me."

Jesus possessed charm. He seemed more concerned to pay attention to others than that they be impressed with Him. He must have listened to thousands.

"Who touched me?" He asked.

The scriptures say, "And she told Him the whole story." He showed His sympathy in healing her. He showed His love in listening to her.

Everybody has a story to tell. A part of my Christian discipleship involves making the effort to listen. But more than this, as I give an understanding ear to another, I get a rest from the constant drumbeat of my own concerns.

PRAYER: O Lord, help us in choir to listen to one another, not as to a patient, but to a human being in need of a supporting friend.
                        In Christ,
                        Amen.

Chapter 45

WHERE ARE THE ROADSIGNS?

> "And he said to him, 'If now I have found favor with thee, then show me a sign that it is thou who speakest with me'."
>
> JUDGES 6:17

"Watch me!" David said. "I will lead you through this tough section, but you must watch me."

Later, reflecting on those instructions, I thought, God makes the same promise. But David's guidance seems easier to discern than God's. Sometimes the haziness of God's will causes me to ask, "Where are his roadsigns?"

It seems He guided others. He sent a sign to Gideon. He spoke to Moses and clearly called the prophets. But He seems to be more shy with me. I give Him time to say anything He might want me to hear, but I never hear His voice and seldom know for sure His word to me. Others may claim some direct line from God, even act as though the Holy Spirit were their personal secretary, but guidance from God is a difficult discipline for me. The lack of a voice from God forces me back to the common resources on which I have depended all my life . . . the Bible, church, and reason.

The Bible helps. I don't use it like a horoscope or a crystal ball but it teaches principles of life which I trust.

I believe God also guides me through the fellowship of the church. Members of the choir support me in what seems to them to be God's will for me.

Most of all, I depend upon my own mind. God's guidance comes through the use of reason and common sense. At times I feel as though God breaks through and touches my consciousness with His. I can't explain it by anything external. It's more internally perceived than intellectually understood, but I have learned to trust it.

If God can guide the swallow and the plover thousands of miles to an unknown home, and can lead the salmon to her spawning bed through uncharted streams, I believe He can also guide me even through the tough sections of my life.

PRAYER: O Lord, we don't ask to hear a voice, but make us aware of Your presence in our choices.
                                      In Christ,
                                      Amen.

Chapter 46

MAXIMUM LIVING

> "And while he was at Bethany in the house of Simon the Leper, as he sat at table a woman came with an alabaster jar of ointment of pure nard, very costly, and she broke the jar and poured it over his head."
>
> MARK 14:3

The card read: SPECIAL REHEARSAL
SATURDAY, 10:00 A.M.
IMPORTANT

Oh, no, I thought. Saturday's chores already overwhelm me. I can't slice out time for a choir rehearsal.

Yet when I joined the choir, I didn't sign up for just the minimum amount. "I'll give it my best," I remember saying. "The church deserves an excellent choir and I want to help it be just that. So if special rehearsals are called for, I'll go, not because I must, but because I'm committed."

My extra effort not only strengthens a better choir, it makes a better me. Minimum living gives no excitement to life.

I remember as a child, I often wondered how little I could get by on. "If I wash my hands, do I have to wash my face also?" or "If I go to Sunday school, do I have to go to church, too?" How little and how much?

As an adult, I know that the fun in life comes after we surpass the minimum requirements. I enjoy most those things to which I give my all. Perhaps this is what Jesus had in mind when He praised the woman who anointed Him with an expensive perfume. He proclaimed her unreserved devotion as something beautiful. Jesus, Himself, gave His all without holding back. Nothing lukewarm about His life commitments.

So I will enjoy the extra rehearsal, not as an obligation, but as an opportunity for abundant living.

PRAYER: O Lord, thank You for our second mile opportunities that we may discover the exciting ventures in life.
In Christ,
Amen.

Chapter 47

WHEN THE LIGHTS GO OUT

> "But now, since I no longer have any room for work in these regions, and since I have longed for many years to come to you, . . ."
> ROMANS 15:23

We had rehearsed for tonight's cantata for more than three months. I had already envisioned the excitement of the choir and congregation. It was going to be our most ambitious performance. The congregation filled the sanctuary and we were ready. Then, the lights went out: a power shortage for the whole area!

Panic! No organ and we couldn't read the music. But we sang anyway . . . to piano and in candlelight, accompanied by thunder and lightning.

The question in life is not *if* we will suffer disappointment but *how*. We all face unfulfilled dreams. The lights go out on us. We cannot choose *when*, only *how* we will react. Some seek to escape the letdowns of life by giving up, getting drunk, or by committing suicide. At times, I too want to run away, but as a Christian, I know there's a better way.

The Apostle Paul had many experiences of lights going out, but he turned life's disappointments into God's opportunities.

On one occasion, he wanted to go to Europe. He wound up in a Roman prison. Even then he called for pen and paper and from his dungeon wrote the letters that make up more than half the New Testament.

As someone said: "When God closes a door, He always opens a

window. God never abandons us with no opportunity to serve Him. Trust answers disappointments. Even when it's dark, I can reach out and join the work of God.

"Honestly," Ellen said, "tonight has to be one of the most inspiring experiences of my life. Listening to the choir sing by candlelight gave me a thrill that could have never been programmed. It was great!"

PRAYER: O Lord, teach us to seek new ways to serve You when the old ones no longer work.
          In Christ,
          Amen.

Chapter 48

YEAH, THAT'S WHAT I SAY

> "Blessed be the Lord, the God of Israel, from everlasting to everlasting! And let all the people say, "Amen!" Praise the Lord!"
>
> PSALM 106:48

"Now, everybody together on the Amen," David said.

Singing the word reminds me of the Psalmist, "And let all the people say, 'Amen'." I like to hear a strong Amen. Yet this most frequent word of worship receives little thought in our day. We say it to announce the end of a prayer or hymn. Its best use in worship has nearly lost its meaning.

The word Amen is a declaration of faith. It means, "So let it be." When I use it, I proclaim my trust in God's promises. It's my agreement and support of all that has gone before. It's a way of saying, "Yes, me too!"

At home I say, "Peanut butter sure is good."

My son responds, "Yeah, that's what I say."

The minister says, "The Lord is good above all else."

We respond, "Yeah, that's what we say." However, being more reserved we simply say, "Amen."

Yet the *Amen* does more than show agreement. It's also an expression of gratitude, emotion and commitment.

For example, when I saw the Grand Canyon for the first time, I gasped. Great music can bring tears to my eyes, or I stand clapping in spontaneous response.

In the same way, when prayer claims a trusting relationship with God, I want to shout, "Amen, that's what I say."

I never want to sing a casual Amen. We may sing a simple one-time Amen or a fancy seven-fold type . . . but never a *careless* Amen. When I sing it, I want the words to be a prayer or hymn of my own. The action of God becomes real to me as I say "Amen." It expresses my faith.

PRAYER: O Lord, let us sing the Amens as an exciting response to Your gracious acts of love for us.
                              In Christ,
                              Amen.

Chapter 49

DANCE A LITTLE

> "And David danced before the Lord with all his might; and David was girded with a linen ephod."
> II SAMUEL 6:14

"Coming to the choir party?" I asked.

"No," Steve answered. "I joined the choir to work and sing for the Lord. I didn't join to play."

I felt a sadness in our quick exchange but I didn't respond.

I believe fellowship and fun meets several longings. "Rejoice always" the Bible says. I think we all want that. Nobody chooses to trudge through life with no parades unless, of course, we confuse duty with sadness or work with value.

Many of us spend most of our time working; if there's time left from work, we play. If we aren't committed to work or play on the weekends, we worship. Someone said, "Americans worship their work, work at their play and play at their worship." Maybe so.

I wish we could put more joy in all three: work, play, and worship. Hospital beds are filled with conscientious workaholics who have lost their zest for life. All work and no play not only makes Jack a dull boy, but robs him of his health and spirit.

On the other hand, exhilarated outbursts of song and thanksgiving periodically overflow the believer's heart. David became so excited by the return of the Ark of the Covenant to Israel that he danced before the Lord.

I like to see my children having a good time. I enjoy their play and laughter. Therefore it's easy to imagine that God, our father, desires joy for His children.

So I go to choir parties. They not only lift morale but I believe God must be pleased when our faith and fellowship also becomes our fun.

PRAYER: O Lord, in the midst of our work, teach us to dance a little.
In Christ,
Amen.

Chapter 50

GOD'S RHYTHM

> "Be still, and know that I am God. I am exalted among the nations, I am exalted in the earth."
> PSALM 46:10

". . . and keep us all safe and well through the night," David prayed and then said to all of us, "Good night, choir, see you Sunday."

As we stood to leave, Neal said, "I don't know why we have to close rehearsal with a prayer. Seems like an empty ceremony to me."

"Don't you believe in prayer?" I asked.

"Hum, yes and no. But I don't think prayer will keep us 'safe through the night,' as David said. It never works for me. I've prayed for better gas mileage and that my team will win the football game. But . . ."

"Are you serious?" I interrupted. "Prayer is not an Aladdin's lamp."

"That's my point," he said. "What's the use?"

Neal came across a little blunt but he raised a question that bothers many of us. What happens when we pray?

Peter was released from prison when the early Christians prayed in the home of Rhoda. Thus, many preachers exhort, "Pray expectantly, God answers prayers made in faith." Yet later, Peter was crucified upside down, in spite of prayer. Why pray, if you can't depend upon it?

I pray for the same reason birds fly or flowers grow. It seems the natural thing to do. In times of need, I pray without question or understanding. The value I feel in prayer has little to do with changing circumstances. I don't pray for results, I pray because of my *relationship* with God.

When praying, I share my life with God and it's in prayer that I feel His presence the strongest. In saying "Be still and know that I am God," the Psalmist affirms a needed rhythm in life.

God calls us to action, to work and make things happen. But He also wants us to retreat, to rest and pray.

For most of us, prayer is not argued out of life but crowded out. We get too busy. We need frequent reminders of God's presence in our lives. Therefore I'm grateful for the moment at the end of rehearsal when David says, "Okay, choir. Good work. Let us pray."

PRAYER: O Lord, we get so busy we fail to pray. Thank You for every quiet moment in which we realize Your presence.
In Christ,
Amen.

Chapter 51

THE RISK OF BEING THERE

> "The eternal God is your dwelling place, and underneath are the everlasting arms."
> DEUTERONOMY 33:27

"Watch your entrances," David said. "One delayed attack spoils the line."

David didn't call my name but I knew he spoke to me. I was late coming in on the first note. Subconsciously I hold back to be sure the others are singing before I start. I have a fear of coming in ahead of the rest and sticking out all alone, so I slip in after the phrase starts. It's risky to attack on time. I have to trust that the others will start with me.

Choir is not the only place I risk depending on others. I did that when I got married, when I let my daughter leave for college, and when I had my appendix out.

We can't live without taking risks because none of us is independent. We must rely on others but sometimes we get let down. Choose the wrong person to trust and we get hurt. Even those who love us cannot always hold us up. Only God forever sustains. "Underneath are the everlasting arms," promises us the only hope that never fades.

So, I put myself into the care of friends who in turn put themselves into my care. In our limited way, we can uphold one another because we know God keeps us all. God is the real gambler. He risks into our hands His good will to all His people. As far as I know, He has no back-up in case we fail.

"Risk being on time," David said. "Trust that if you give it your best, others will be there with you."

"Trust me," Bob whispered. "I'll come in with you. Besides, risk is what makes singing in a choir exciting."

"Yeah," I replied. "The same is true of life."

PRAYER: O Lord, remind us of Your everlasting arms that we may risk falling in order to sustain one another.
                         In Christ,
                         Amen.

Chapter 52

ON SAYING GOODBYE

> ". . . be content with what you have; for he has said, 'I will never fail you nor forsake you'."
>
> HEBREWS 13:5

"Transferred!" I almost shouted.

"That's right," Bob answered. "We move next month." When Bob announced his leaving, I felt sick. We had been close. We often shared problems, worked and vacationed together. It seemed he had always been in choir with me. I don't say "goodbye" very well, especially to a friend of seventeen years.

Saying hello feels good but goodbye hurts. We promise to keep in touch, to write and visit.

"Why, we'll be back," he said. We both knew better. It would never be the same.

I tried to look on the bright side. Bob's new job represented a promotion, but it also robbed us of the security of a proven friendship. We both grieved through our smiles.

Saying goodbye to Bob reminds me that nothing lasts, no matter how good. Peter once begged, "Lord, can't we stay here? We don't want to leave." Jesus refused his effort to enshrine the past. In another incident, Jesus warned that anyone trying to keep life means relinquishing it. By letting go we find; by holding on, we lose. We cannot cling to yesterday and still reach for what is yet to be.

I can cherish our past friendship without being imprisoned by it. The past was never complete. Some things need to be forgiven, others erased and still others remembered with appreciation. All those mixed feelings to carry me into the future.

The security of the past can give me the courage to change. This is true of my friendship with Bob, but it's also true of my relationship with God. God with me in the past gives me confidence to trust Him in the future. I usually think of God above me, but I sometimes think of God *ahead* of me.

Every relationship dies eventually . . . except mine and God's.

PRAYER: O Lord, help us to hear Your promise to never leave nor forsake us.
                          In Christ,
                          Amen.

Chapter 53

THANKSGIVING – A MATTER OF FAITH

> "... always and for everything giving thanks in the name of our Lord Jesus Christ to God the Father."
> EPHESIANS 5:20

"I wish Thanksgiving didn't come at the end of the year," Bob said. "I'm too busy to be thankful."

"It tempts me to be thankful for the wrong things," I said. "Thanksgiving in November implies that we look back and express gratitude for all our past blessings. Like wise owls, we sit as judges over past events to determine what will and what won't be included in our prayers of Thanksgiving."

"Well, is that wrong?" Bob asked.

"What about those who have not been blessed?" I asked. "The Dells will celebrate today's meal with an empty chair at the table. Sam spent most of last year struggling with his illness. What does Thanksgiving say to them? 'Cheer up, it could have been worse?'"

"I don't know," Bob said. "And I'm too busy to think about it."

But I couldn't stop thinking about it. Paul said, "Always and for everything giving thanks." It's easy to be thankful for the good that comes to me . . . but for everything? Is Paul asking us to peek under every misfortune to find some hidden blessing there? I could do that, I guess. If I break my toe, I could be thankful that it wasn't my leg, but I hope Paul spoke of a more healthy attitude.

I believe genuine Thanksgiving is not so dependent upon outward circumstances. It's a set of the soul. Thanksgiving grows out of a deep sense of the close goodness of God.

It's not so much what God does *for* us, as what God does *in* us. Thanksgiving expresses a confidence in God's love over all the misfortunes of the world.

PRAYER: O Lord, give us confidence in Your presence with us in all things and make us grateful.
> In Christ,
> Amen.

Chapter 54

CHRISTMAS – RUSH, RUSH, RUSH

> "A voice cries: 'In the wilderness prepare the way of the Lord, make straight in the desert a highway for our God'."
>
> ISAIAH 40:3

"I'll be glad when it's over," Lillian said. "No good can come from all this rush, rush, rush. I still have cards to write, gifts to mail, meals to prepare and a crib to borrow and I'm already worn out!"

Holidays have a tendency to degenerate. The season to remember the birth of Christ becomes two weeks of overeating, office parties and a free day to sleep it off.

But what would I change? Would I have us cut down on the shopping? That would mean fewer gifts and who would I leave out? Would Christmas be improved by reducing our generosity?

Maybe I'd control the music, blaring out at us from every street corner, too much and too loud. But could I really build a spirit of Christmas if there were no carols or music where people gather? Even the lights and decorations contribute to the lifting of the mood.

Some say, "Cut out the appeals for charity. Eliminate the soft touch. Forget Christmas baskets. At least we could cut out so much cooking and travel and Santa Claus, trees, and greens."

No, I wouldn't cut out any of these things. One of the glories of

Christmas is that it's not celebrated in a closet. I don't have to protect it from the explosion of human reaction to such Good News. Everybody, not just Christians, celebrates Christmas and I am glad.

I fear if we take all the frenzy out of the preparation for Christmas, we'd lose it, unless of course we change human nature. Substitute a soft mood, withdraw from the world, pray and contemplate God and Christmas would become as little known as Epiphany.

"Prepare the way," Isaiah said. Let us not hold back because some of the preparations are not religious.

Christmas is too big not to spill over into the whole secular world.

PRAYER: O Lord, we are glad for the world's celebration of the birth of Christ. Catch us up in all the excitement of this season.

                In Christ,
                Amen.

Chapter 55

NEW YEARS – ONE DAY AT A TIME

> "This is the day which the Lord has made; let us rejoice and be glad in it."
> PSALM 118:24

"I wish I had this year to live over," Ron said at our New Year's Eve Service. "I'd like to have another try at it."

"Not I," I said, "I may not do as well the second time. In fact, I escaped some consequences I deserved."

Later I laughed . . . what an idiotic exchange. Yesterday is gone no matter how we feel about it. As someone said, "Yesterday is a cancelled check; tomorrow is a promissory note. All the cash you have is today."

One day at a time offers me all I can manage. If God gave me two at once, I'd probably drown in them. To be agreeable, kind and loving for one day is all I can handle. Mental institutions are filled with those who try to carry today the guilt of yesterday or the anxiety of tomorrow.

We live in today. I believe God forgives my yesterday. He forgets it, and what He forgets, I can forget. I don't honor Him by clinging to old garbage.

Neither do I show faith by fretting about tomorrow. Most of the things that have changed my life hardly related to my plans or fears. They came to me as bonuses. I can trust God's love to hold all my tomorrows.

"This is the day which the Lord has made; let us rejoice and be glad in it." The Psalmist calls me to a decision.

Between the nostalgia of "Auld Lang Syne" and the hope for years to come, I will seek my life. I will live it, not by the lifetime, nor the year, but by the day.

PRAYER: O Lord, forgive our failings of yesterday, and reassure us of Your care in tomorrow, that we may enjoy Your presence with us today.
In Christ,
Amen.

Chapter 56

EPIPHANY – GOING HOME DIFFERENT

> "And being warned in a dream not to return to Herod, they departed to their own country by another way."
> MATTHEW 2:12

"Christmas is finally over," I overheard Eleanor say. "When the kids return to school, things will get back to normal again."

I'm afraid she's right. Too soon things will get back like they were. That disturbs me. Christmas should make a difference. After the decorations have been stored away and the tree carried off by the trash truck, I should never see it as finally over.

The wise men, after seeing the Christ child, "departed to their own country by another way." Obviously they were avoiding Herod. But they were changed, too. No one could experience the birth of Christ and be the same.

The world pressures us to leave the Christmas experience behind. It assures us that "peace on earth, good will toward men" cannot survive beyond the emotions of a few holy days.

"Do not be conformed to this world," Paul said, "but be transformed." Christ makes us different.

I believe if we experience Christmas, it will transform us. He came that we might face life in a new way. Christmas assures us that the distance between God and us has been bridged. He walks into a new year with us.

So I hope things never return to "normal." Rather, having seen the Christmas child, we can take a different way. If Christmas does not create in us the courage to change, to make things better, then Christ came in vain.

As the choir prepares to sing its music, I want to help proclaim that Christmas brings a life-changing message. When we sing the well-known hymn, "Go Tell It On the Mountain," I want its message imprinted on my heart so that it will influence me the rest of the year.

PRAYER: O Lord, now that the season is over, make us aware of the spirit of Christmas that lingers. Send us home a different way, even now.
In Christ,
Amen.

Chapter 57

MISSIONS – IMPRACTICAL

> "Jesus said, 'They need not go away; you give them something to eat.' They said to him, 'We have only five loaves here and two fish'."
>
> MATTHEW 14:16-17

"Jesus asked only for what they had," Reverend Walker said. "Today we will take an offering for missions."

I understand how Philip, the disciple, felt. The job was too big. It must have looked like the whole world out there. There was no way for Jesus and His disciples to feed that crowd. Two hundred denari represented half a year's pay. "Send the crowds away," Philip said. Furthermore, Jesus had come to this place to rest, not to confront five thousand people. Sometimes I also want to send them away.

I believe in missions but we must be practical. We offer all kinds of reasons. Our church is caught in an economic crunch. Money doesn't have the buying power it once had. The credit syndrome has us operating in debt. It's hard to know how much we can afford. We built this church to meet our needs first.

I love the fellowship. Philip did, too. He appreciated Jesus and had left all to be with Him. He knew Jesus' need to be available to all people, but Philip wanted private time. That's why they crossed the sea, but all those people followed. Enough was enough. The crowd's intrusion made him say, "We can't possibly feed all of them."

Sometimes I also want private time. I love my church, especially the choir. My friends are here and I appreciate the work and love we share. I belong. So I don't want to hear about hungry people. I don't want my fellowship threatened by the intruding needs of others. They'll have to take care of themselves. We can't possibly care for everyone.

Then Andrew came, an impractical dreamer with no sense of the problem. "Lord, there is a lad here who has five barley loaves and two fish." And with that, Jesus fed them all. He took only *what they had* and worked a miracle with it.

Day by day I tend to live by the prudence of Philip. But every now and then, God nudges me to be impractical, to take an uncalculated leap of faith like Andrew.

I don't understand miracles, but I believe Jesus can take what we have and multiply it for the needs of others.

PRAYER: O Lord, help us as a choir to see beyond the problems and become partners with You in missions.
In Christ,
Amen.

Chapter 58

PALM SUNDAY – EXPECTING TOO LITTLE

> "And those who went before, and those who followed cried out, 'Hosanna! Blessed is he who comes in the name of the Lord! Blessed is the kingdom of our father David that is coming! Hosanna in the highest.' And he entered Jerusalem, and went into the temple; and when he had looked around at everything, as it was already late, he went out to Bethany with the twelve."
>
> MARK 11:9-11

"Altos, watch for the major chord ending," David said. "If you don't expect it, you may miss it."

An appropriate warning, I thought, especially for Palm Sunday. Two thousand years ago, they didn't expect Jesus.

The crowds gathered, shouting, singing and waving palm branches before Him. Their King, God's chosen One, arrived. They followed Him through the city to an open place before the temple. Jesus dismounted. The crowd watched His every move. They scanned the sky for a sign. Any moment now He would call in a mighty stream of men, horses and ships to establish the Kingdom of Israel forever.

They watched Him go into the temple. *Nothing!* Time passed and still nothing. One by one the crowd melted away with no more than an empty feeling. No wonder they crucified Him; Jesus was not what they expected.

They wanted a king they could believe in. Instead, He came a Christ who believed in them. They wanted Him to fight, He came to love. They missed Him, not because they expected too much, but because they expected too little. They wanted a temporal, earthly Kingdom. He ushered in an eternal, heavenly one.

I often react like the crowd. For instance I struggle with the divinity of Christ. "How could He be God and come riding on a donkey?" I once asked Reverend Walker.

"The importance of the divinity of Christ is not so much that Jesus was God. The significant thing to us is that God was Jesus," he said. "He did not remain up there aloof, but came to us. God on a donkey bridges the gap."

"Thanks," I said. "That's the major chord of Palm Sunday. But like those in Jerusalem, I often miss it. God coming to me is so much more than I expect."

PRAYER: O Lord, we sing Hosanna because You have come to us with Good News. Help us to hear it in spite of our struggle to believe it.
>In Christ,
>Amen.

Chapter 59

EASTER – OUR BIG ONE

> "If Christ has not been raised, your faith is futile and you are still in your sins. Then those also who have fallen asleep in Christ have perished. If for this life only we have hoped in Christ, we are of all men most to be pitied."
> I CORINTHIANS 15:17-19

"Look at that crowd," Earl whispered. "They come on Easter and we won't see them again until next year."

"You may be right," I said. "But I'm glad they're here. If they come only on one day, I'm glad they picked today. This is our big one."

"But," he said, "they come to see friends and show off their new clothes. It irks me."

All during the service, I thought of what Earl had said. I don't agree with him. I'm convinced that underneath any desire to display a wardrobe each person came out of a sincere longing for life. In spite of miracle drugs and space age science, every time we attend a funeral, we know that somewhere down the road, "That'll be me."

No matter how sophisticated we seem publically, privately we ask, "If a man die, shall he live again?"

Our hunger for hope beyond the grave makes this the biggest Sunday of the year. Easter sings a message of a resurrection.

If there is no eternal dimension, then life loses its worth. Values blur and human personality holds no dignity. If death ends all, why care? Why worship or even bother with God? If death destroyed the most perfect life ever lived, then what matters how we live? It'll soon be over and gone forever. Paul said, "If Christ has not been raised, your faith is futile and you are still in your sins. Then those also who have fallen asleep in Christ have perished. If for this life only we have hoped in Christ, we are of all men most to be pitied." That's why Easter is the core of the Christian faith.

So today I'll sing with more enthusiasm than ever before. Maybe those who come only on this Sunday will catch a feeling of the hope this one day proclaims.

PRAYER: O Lord, thank You for the opportunity we have to proclaim the Good News. Help those who see and hear us this day to have a greater faith in Your love.
                    In Christ,
                    Amen.

Chapter 60

PENTECOST – THE SPIRIT AMONG US

> "But the fruit of the Spirit is love, joy, peace, patience, kindness, goodness, faithfulness, gentleness, self-control;"
> GALATIANS 5:22-23

"I guess Pentecost is something good for the church," Mary said, "but I'm not sure I want it."

"I know I don't," an alto responded. "My aunt claims to be 'spirit-filled' and frankly, nobody can get along with her."

"Some churches advertise that they are filled with the Spirit. They speak in tongues. I'm not sure I understand them but they get pretty excited about it," Fred added.

"The Spirit is of God," Ted said softly. "Whatever that means, I want it available to me."

"It seems to me," I said, "we miss the mark when we talk about possessing the Spirit. He's not like Aladdin's lamp, so that if we rub Him with our prayers he'll appear to do our wishes. The Spirit is our Lord, not our servant. He wants to possess us."

For twenty minutes, we asked questions about the Holy Spirit. All of us realized how unsure we felt about this part of our Christian experience.

One thing seems clear to me. The Spirit lives among us. He's never anyone's private property. I fear some who have the gift of the Spirit sometimes use it to lead or force others to have the same kind of experience. They divide us into first and second class Christians. Their air of superiority leads to factions of resentment.

Paul said the fruit of the spirit is, "Love, joy, peace, patience, kindness, goodness, faithfulness, gentleness and self-control." In short, the Spirit creates a fellowship . . . like I sometimes feel in our choir.

"It's amazing," David said to us, "when we work hard, a certain spirit enters into our singing and we actually do better than we have a right to do. The whole is more than the sum of its parts."

I believe that "more" is akin to the Spirit of Pentecost and it creates a bond of oneness among us.

PRAYER: O Lord, fill us with the Spirit of your love that we may experience a unity like the love of that first Pentecost.
In Christ,
Amen.